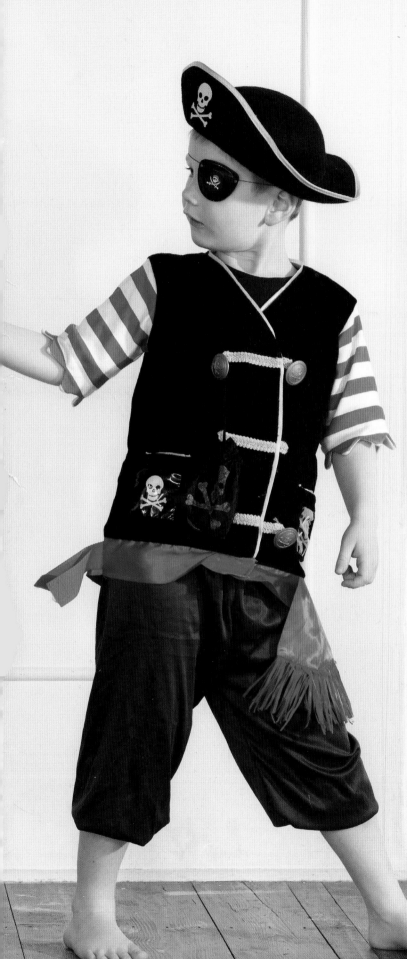

CONTENTS

Introduction 2

Tools and Materials 3

Felt Polly Parrot 4

Eye Patch and Monogrammed Hat 8

Secret Treasure Chest 12

Felt Treasure Map 16

Captain's Hook 20

First Mate's Telescope 24

Pirate Ship Pen Pot 28

Buccaneer Boots 32

Cutlass and Belt 36

Fish for Loot Game 40

Easy-Sew Waistcoat 44

Jolly Roger Flag 48

Pirate Ship 52

Pirate Party 54

Treasure Chest Cake 58

Templates 62

INTRODUCTION

Ahoy there, land lubbers! Do you have a little person who loves nothing more than to set up ship and play pirates all day? Then you've picked up the right book! These pages are packed to the gunnels with a whole heap of crafts to allow you to create everything your little pirate needs. From the monogrammed hat right down to the buckled boots, children are kitted out to be the captain of their own vessel. Once all the accessories are made, we show you how to throw the ultimate pirate party, with games, nibbles, and a glorious treasure chest chocolate cake to sink your teeth into.

And you don't need to worry about complicated tutorials, because the projects have been created with beginner crafters in mind. Each one has clear instructions with photographs to guide you through the steps. There are handy tips throughout, templates at the back for each project that needs them, and stitch guides for the sewn makes.

Most of the projects are intended to be made by adults with their children. Kids can get stuck in and personalize the projects, but some parts will be a little tricky for them to do by themselves—and the end result will be a lot more durable with adult help.

Our kids love everything pirate related and we're regularly instructed to walk the plank or engage in a sword fight. Our favorite thing of all is to make a little personalized map and go on a pirate treasure hunt. So all the projects in the book already have our own kids' swashbuckling seal of approval.

We hope you enjoy making the projects in this book as much as we did, and that your little buccaneer enjoys many treasure-filled sea adventures. We apologize if you have to scrub the decks and walk the plank 100 times a day from now on... we know, we've been there!

TOOLS AND MATERIALS

This section provides an overview of all the basic craft supplies, tools, and bits and bobs you will need for the projects in this book. We have tried to ensure that the materials used throughout are inexpensive and easy to purchase.

Essential supplies

These materials are a must for the projects in this book, and are handy for crafting in general. You probably have most of them already, so have a look through your stocks and bundle them all up together in a box or cupboard. Easy access is useful for crafting with impatient kids!

Paints and brushes

Throughout the book we have used acrylic paint on projects to give them a better quality and more durable finish. Child-friendly paint can be used, but it will require more coats for an even coverage. Paintbrushes in a few different sizes are also needed.

Duct tape

We love this versatile craft material. It comes in a range of colors and patterns, and it's strong, cheap, and mess free.

Plaster of Paris

This is a fantastic material for making heavier-weight, sturdy items. Simply add water to the plaster, then pour it into a mold and leave it to harden. If you want a bespoke shape (as for the Pen Pot, page 28), you will need to make your own mold using sheets of acetate and masking tape.

Other essentials

· Glue—PVA, glue stick, and strong glue
· Craft foam
· Colored and metallic card
· Masking tape
· Double-sided tape
· Permanent marker pens in a range of colors.

It is also useful to keep a box of old containers, boxes, bottles, cups, and tubes that you might otherwise throw out. Having a stash of goodies is a fantastic way to get your children's imaginations flowing, and these could end up being turned into wonderful pirate creations. Keep hold of any corrugated card too; you can make anything from a cutlass (page 36) to a pirate ship (page 52) with the help of a cardboard box.

Sewing supplies
Sewing machine

This is essential for the Waistcoat (page 44) and is useful for making the Polly Parrot and Jolly Roger Flag (pages 4 and 48).

Fabric

Felt is a fantastic fabric as it comes in lots of colors, the edges don't fray, and it's inexpensive.

Iron-on adhesive

Fusible webbing is like magic for materials! It is an iron-on adhesive that sticks two pieces of fabric together, so you don't have to sew them.

Embellishments and trims

Bias binding, embroidery thread, Velcro (hook-and-loop tape), elastic, and buttons all feature in this book.

FELT POLLY PARROT

This pretty Polly makes a great shipmate and a lovely companion for your shoulder. Our parrot has been made with a sewing machine, but she can easily be stitched by hand too. Felt is a great material to work with—it's brightly colored, inexpensive, and the edges don't fray. Polly is compatible with the Waistcoat on page 44, but with a little Velcro (hook-and-loop tape) you can create a perch for her on any top or jumper.

You will need

 1 x sheet each of yellow, red and blue felt, 8 x 12in (20 x 30cm)

 Scraps of black and white felt

 Handful of toy stuffing

 Scissors

 Red, yellow, white, and blue sewing thread, pins and sewing machine

 Yellow and black embroidery thread

 Embroidery needle

 Velcro

Step 1

Photocopy and cut out the templates on page 62, then cut the following pieces from felt:

2 x body pieces in yellow felt
2 x wing pieces in blue felt
2 x eye pieces in white felt
2 x beak pieces in black felt
1 x belly piece in yellow felt
2 x outer tail feathers in red felt
2 x middle tail feathers in blue felt
2 x inner tail feathers in yellow felt

Step 2

To create Polly's tail feathers, use contrasting thread to sew two rows of equally spaced stitches along the length of each feather.

Step 3

Layer the feathers together with the big feather at the bottom and the smallest at the top, and line up the top edges. Pin and sew together ¼in (6mm) from the top. Repeat for the other set of feathers, making sure the two sets are mirror images of each other.

Step 4

Sew the tail feathers onto the body piece along the existing stitch line at the top of the feathers. See the photo for where to place the feathers. Pin the wings onto the body piece above the feathers so the top of the feathers are under the wings and sew along the top curved edge.

Step 5

Pin and sew the white eye piece onto both of the body pieces using white thread. Pin each beak piece onto the inside of the body pieces with a ¼in (6mm) overlap and topstitch using yellow thread.

Step 6

Use black embroidery thread to handsew an eye onto the middle of the white eye piece; sew overlapping crosses to create a star.

Step 7

Pin the belly piece to one of the body pieces with the edges lined up and use yellow embroidery thread to handstitch the two pieces together using blanket stitch (see page 51 for stitch instructions).

Step 8

Pin and stitch the other body piece to the other side of the belly piece with the edges lined up again. Stitch the two body pieces together where they meet, stopping once you reach the beak.

Step 9

Fill the parrot with stuffing until she is plump. Use black embroidery thread to blanket stitch the beak together neatly. Sew a square of Velcro to Polly's bottom to enable her to perch on the waistcoat (see page 44).

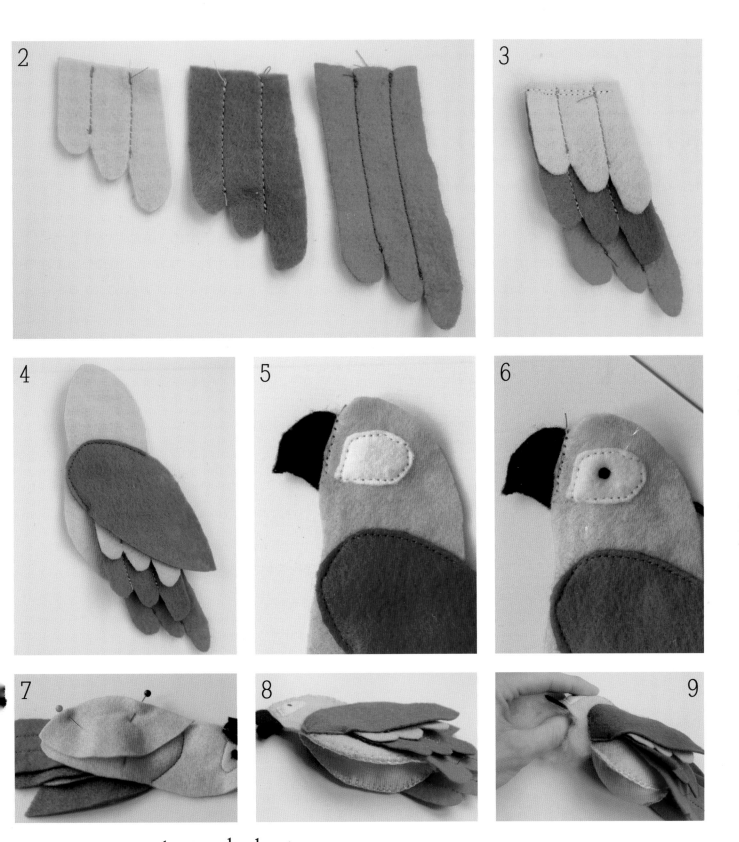

Remember that the two body pieces need to be mirror images
of each other when pinning on the parrot's features.

EYE PATCH AND MONOGRAMMED HAT

No pirate's outfit is complete without an eye patch and hat, and these two are very simple to make from some craft foam and card. Craft foam is a great material to work with, as it's easy to cut out with scissors and is more hard-wearing and water-resistant than card.

You will need

For the eye patch

 1 x sheet black craft foam 3 x 4in (8 x 10cm)

 1 x sheet white craft foam 3 x 4in (8 x 10cm)

 Sharp scissors

 Hole punch

 Pin

 Pencil

 Strong glue

 Sewing needle

 12in (30cm) length of thin elastic

For the hat

 2 x sheets of black card, 12 x 16in (30 x 40cm)

 1 x sheet of white card, 8 x 12in (20 x 30cm)

 1 x sheet of black craft foam, 12 x 16in (30 x 40cm)

 1 x sheet of gold card, 8 x 12in (20 x 30cm)

 Pencil

 Scissors or craft knife

 Glue stick

 Sewing needle

 Tape measure

 Stapler

Step 1

Photocopy and cut out the templates for the eye patch and the skull and crossbones on pages 62–63. Cut the eye patch from the black foam and the skull and two bones from the white foam. Use a hole punch to cut out the skull eyes and use a pin to make the nose—give it a wiggle to make it a bit bigger.

Step 2

Arrange the skull and crossbones onto the eye patch as shown in the picture. On one of the bones, mark where it crosses over and cut out the middle section to enable it to lie flat either side of the other bone. Glue in place.

Step 3

Use a needle to pierce the holes on each side of the eye patch, as marked on the template.

Step 4

Thread the elastic through one of the holes, secure with a knot, and trim off any excess. Thread the other end through the other hole, check the fit on your child's head, and knot in place.

Step 5

For the hat, use the template on page 62 to draw and cut two hat shapes from the black card. Place the template on one half of the card, then flip it over to draw the other half.

Step 6

Use the skull and crossbones template on page 62 to draw and cut out a skull and two bones from the white card.

Step 7

Draw the child's initials onto a piece of paper (or print them out), no bigger than 2½in (6cm) high, to create a template. Draw around them onto the remaining white card and cut out. Glue the skull and crossbones onto the middle of one of the hat pieces and glue the letters on either side of the skull.

Step 8

Use a tape measure to measure the circumference of your child's head. Cut a 2in (5cm) strip of foam to this length, adding an extra ½in (1cm) for overlap. Staple the two ends together, with the sharp edges of the staples facing out.

Step 9

Staple the foam strip onto the back of one of the hat pieces, at the top and bottom of the foam (again with the sharp edges facing out). Repeat for the other piece, lining up the edges of the card.

Step 10

Staple the side edges of the hat together. Cut the bottom strip off the template and use it as a template to cut two strips of gold card. Arrange along the bottom edge of the hat and glue in place.

You could also use self-adhesive foam for the skull and crossbones; this is easy to find in most craft shops.

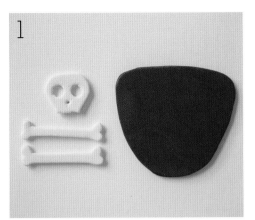

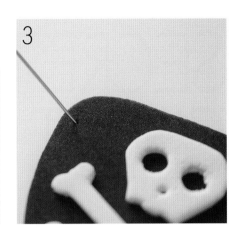

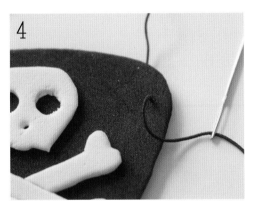

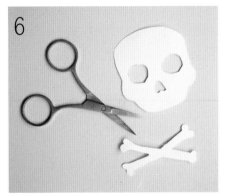

SECRET TREASURE CHEST

This cardboard treasure chest is the perfect place to hide all your valuable jewels, coins, and trinkets. It's made from a shoebox and a little bit of papier mâché and comes with its own secret compartment, hidden in the lid. Perfect for hoarding your extra-special booty away from fellow shipmates!

You will need

 1 x cardboard shoebox, about 12in (30cm) long

 1 x cardboard box, about 4 x 3 x 1½in (10 x 8 x 4cm); a small cereal box works well

 3 x sheets of card, 8 x 12in (20 x 30cm)

 3½ x ¾in (9 x 2cm) strip of Velcro (hook-and-loop tape)

 1 sheet of black craft foam, 12 x 16in (30 x 40cm)

 1 x sheet of gold card, 8 x 12in (20 x 30cm)

 8 x 12in (20 x 30cm) foam board

 Black marker pen

 Scissors and craft knife

 Masking tape

 Double-sided tape

 Newspaper

 PVA glue and water

 Brown and gold acrylic paints

 Paintbrushes

 Gold duct tape

 Strong glue

 Hole punch

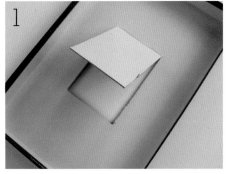

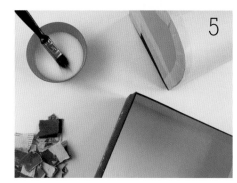

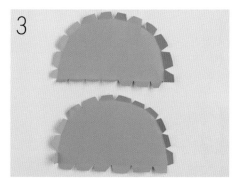

Step 1

Begin by making the secret compartment (shhh!). Take the shoebox lid and, in the center on the inside, draw around the large side of the small box (laid down flat) in the middle. Use a craft knife to cut along the two long sides and one of the short sides to create a door on the lid. Lightly score the remaining side so that it folds easily.

Step 2

Cut the center out of one of the large sides of the small box, ½in (1cm) from the edge, using a craft knife. Cut into the corners to create four tabs and bend them backwards, then line it up with the door on top of the lid and hold it in place with masking tape.

Step 3

Draw a dome shape onto card. The base should be the same width as the lid, and about 7in (18cm) high. Draw around the dome, adding about ½in (1cm) all the way around. Cut tabs all around the curved edge of the dome about 1in (2.5cm) apart and fold in. Repeat this step so you have two domes.

Step 4

Trim the two remaining pieces of card so they are the same length as the lid of the box, if required. Use double-sided tape to stick the card together lengthways. Then attach this to the tabs of the dome by putting a strip of double-sided tape down each side of the card. Start at one end of the dome and gently press each side of the card onto each dome. Cut off any excess card once you reach the other side of the dome.

Step 5

Make the papier mâché paste by mixing two cups of PVA glue to one cup of water. Tear up newspaper into roughly 1in (2.5cm) square pieces. Mark on the box with pen where the rim of the lid comes to, then remove the lid. Spread a thin layer of paste onto a section of the box, then cover that section with newspaper. Repeat this all the way around the outside of the box, stopping at the lid line you marked. Cover the outside of the lid the same way, then leave to dry overnight. You can add one or two more layers of papier mâché to create extra strength if needed.

Step 6

Paint the outside of the box brown; you may need several coats for an even coverage. Cover the inside of the secret compartment in gold duct tape.

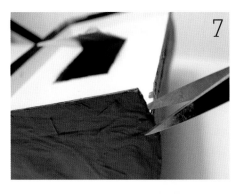

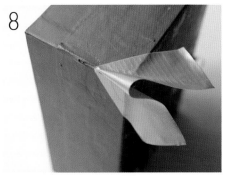

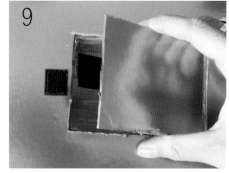

Step 7

Decide which side will be the front of the box, then snip open the lid at the back so that it hinges open when attached. Glue inside the back of the lid and stick onto the box. Strengthen it on the inside with gold duct tape. Paint the inside of the chest gold.

Step 8

Take about 7in (18cm) of gold duct tape and fold it around one of the bottom corners of the box to create a triangular gilded corner. Repeat for all the corners on the box and the front corners of the lid. Cut away the excess tape.

Step 9

To secure the secret compartment, cut a ¾in (2cm) strip of the hook side of the Velcro and a 2½in (6cm) strip of the loop side. Glue the smaller piece next to where the compartment opens on the lid. Line up the loop and hook pieces, and glue the end of the loop piece inside the compartment door.

Step 10

To make the straps, cut two 1½in (3.5cm) wide strips of black foam long enough to wrap over the lid and overlap the opening a little. Round off the edges with scissors on one end of each piece. Use a hole punch to make four holes, 1in (2.5cm) apart, in the middle at the rounded end. Cut two buckles from gold card, using the template on page 62, and

slide onto the end. Use double-sided tape to attach the straps and buckle onto the lid of the box, each one about 1in (2.5cm) from the side. Cut a keyhole from gold card, using the template on p62, and glue to the front of the lid.

Step 11

Decorate the sides of the chest using black permanent marker pen. This version features a diamond pattern, but you could do anything you like. You could even personalize the chest with your pirate's initials.

Step 12

Finally, to make the coins, cut out 3in (8cm) circles from foam board. Paint them gold and leave them to dry, then decorate with coin markings and numbers using permanent black marker pen.

When using a craft knife, put a craft mat under your box to prevent damage to the work surface.

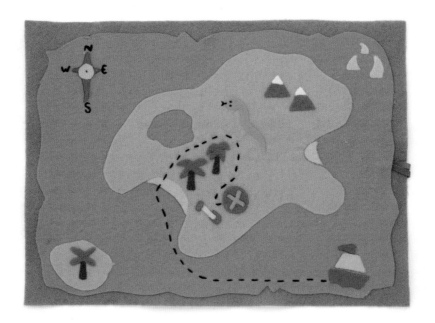

FELT TREASURE MAP

This map (and maybe a spade...) is all you need for a proper treasure hunt adventure. It's made from felt, making it durable and reusable, so you can keep it with all your pirate goodies ready for a day of swashbuckling fun. You could even adapt the map to show things in your own back garden, and stitch it to show a real route leading to actual treasure.

You will need

 1 x sheet of plain paper, 8 x 12in (20 x 30cm)

 1 x sheet each of green, blue and brown felt, 8 x 12in (20 x 30cm)

 Scraps of felt in a mix of other colors (such as yellow, red, white and green)

 2 x pieces fusible webbing, 8 x 12in (20 x 30cm)

 16in (40cm) length of suede strip or ribbon, about ¼in (6mm) thick

 Black marker pen

 Muslin cloth and iron

 20in (50cm) length of black embroidery thread

 Embroidery needle

 Pins

1

2

Step 1

Begin by drawing a map onto the plain paper. You can trace the templates provided (see page 64) or draw your own map features. Remember these will need to be cut from felt, so keep the shapes fairly simple.

Step 2

Pin the map onto the green felt and cut around the island(s).

Step 3

Roughly cut all the other shapes out from the paper island and sea to create templates. Pin these onto the felt and carefully cut out the pieces.

Step 4

For any shapes made up of two colors, first pin onto one color of felt, cut out that part, then use the remaining paper template to cut out the other piece.

Step 5

Place the felt pieces onto the back of a sheet of fusible webbing and draw around them. Cut out and iron onto the back of the felt as per the manufacturer's instructions. Note that your iron may melt the fabric, so place the felt under a muslin cloth and iron on top of the cloth.

Step 6

Remove the backing from the fusible webbing and arrange the felt pieces onto the blue sheet of felt. Make sure the pieces are at least ½in (1cm) from the edge of the fabric. Use the muslin cloth again and iron the pieces in place onto the map.

Step 7

Tie a knot in the end of the embroidery thread. Use a needle to stitch a route using running stitch around the map to the treasure. If you like, you can stitch points on a compass and features on the snake, or any other features you have added. Tie the thread on the back of the fabric to secure it at the end.

Step 8

Cut around the map to make the edges look weathered, about ½in (1cm) from the edge.

Step 9

Draw around the map onto a piece of fusible webbing. Cut out and iron on to the back of the map to set (use a muslin cloth over the top as in Step 5). Remove the backing, then fold the ribbon in half and place the folded end onto one of the narrow sides of the back of the map, in the center. Place the sheet of brown felt on top and iron to secure, sealing in the ribbon.

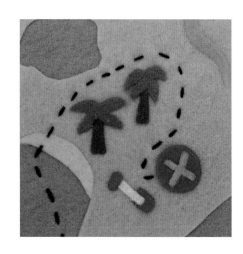

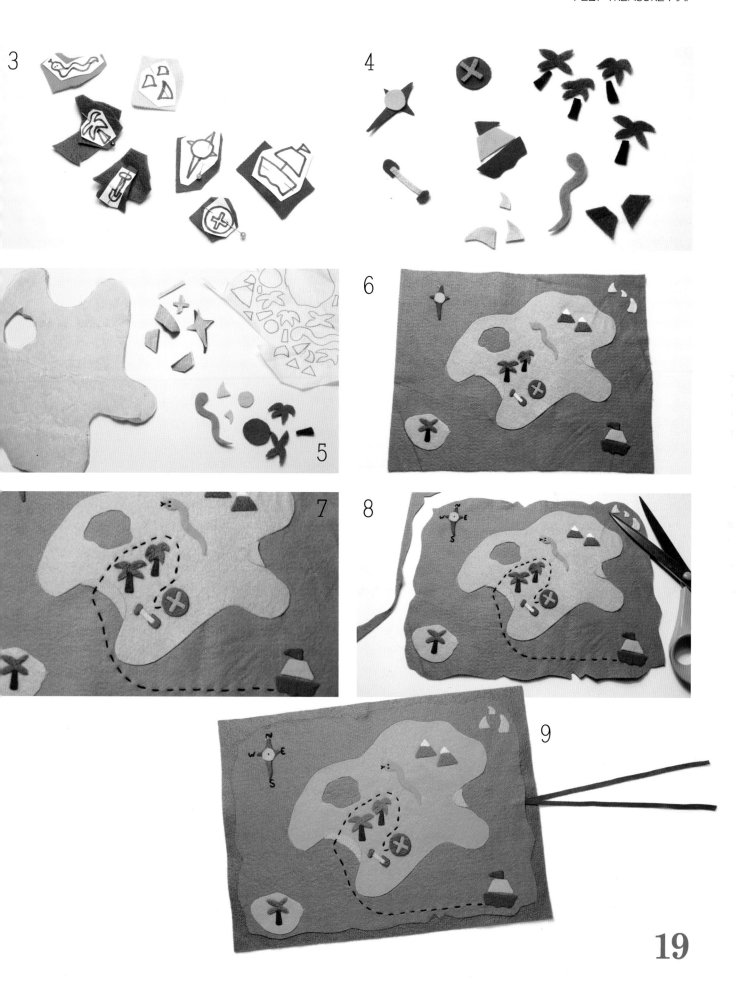

CAPTAIN'S HOOK

This pirate hook is made using the end of a plastic bottle, wire, and duct tape. It has a handle on the inside so that children can hold onto it and disguise their hand.

You will need

 Wire coat hanger

 3½-pint (2-litre) plastic bottle

 Handful of moldable clay

 3 or 4 large sheets of newspaper

 Craft foam

 Wire cutters

 Marker pen

 Scissors

 Masking tape

 PVA glue (2 cups)

 Water (1 cup)

 Silver duct tape

 Paintbrush

Red and black acrylic paints

Tape measure

Pencil

Step 1

First, cut off the hook from the coat hanger. Mark a line 2in (5cm) from the center of the hanger on both sides and use wire cutters to cut it off. Twist the two ends together.

Step 2

Discard the lid from the plastic bottle and mark 5in (13cm) down from the rim. Draw a line all around the bottle at this point and use scissors to cut along it.

Step 3

Fill the neck of the bottle with moldable clay and push the coat hanger through the top. Just the hook part should be visible through the top of the bottle, with the rest of the wire inside (this will be used as the handle).

Step 4

Use masking tape to cover the top and bottom of the bottle top to keep the hook in place.

Step 5

Make up some papier-mâché paste by mixing two parts PVA to one part water and then tearing up pieces of newspaper to make roughly 1in (2.5cm) squares.

Step 6

Spread glue onto the plastic bottle and place the newspaper pieces on top. Then spread glue on top of the newspaper and cover the inside and outside of the hook, making sure there are no gaps.

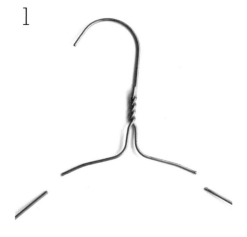

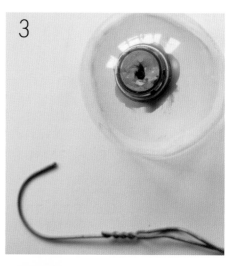

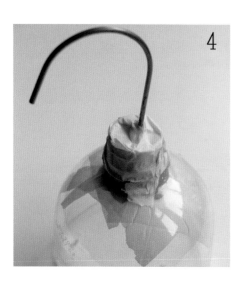

Step 7

Draw around the hook onto the foam, adding ¼in (6mm) onto either side. Repeat this to create two foam hooks, then place them on either side of the wire hook and tape in place with silver duct tape.

Step 8

Paint the base of the hook red.

Step 9

Once dry, measure ½in (1cm) from the bottom and use a tape measure and pencil to mark a line all the way around. Add three more lines, each ¼in (6mm) above the previous, in order to create two stripes.

Step 10

Carefully paint the stripes black.

Step 11

For decoration, use the black paint to create small triangles just under the neck of the bottle.

Step 12

Finally, wrap duct tape around the wire in the center of the bottle several times to create a comfortable padded handle.

7

8

9
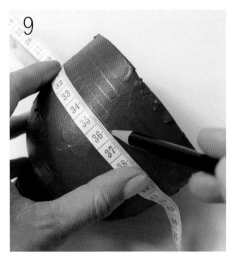

10
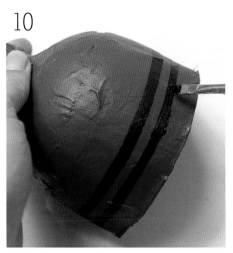

11

12
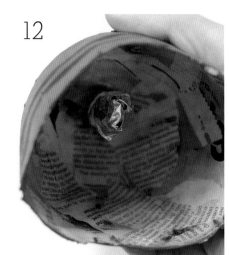

FIRST MATE'S TELESCOPE

Land ahoy! Pirates will easily be able to spot intruder ships with this cardboard tube telescope, which makes it one of the most important pieces of equipment on a pirate ship. This telescope is extra special because it comes complete with its own seascape drawn inside.

You will need

 1 x cardboard cup, about 4½ x 3½in (11 x 9cm)

 1 x cardboard tube, about 4½ x 2in (11 x 5cm)

 1 x sheet of acetate, about 3in (8cm) square

 1 x sheet of gold card, 8 x 12in (20 x 30cm)

 Permanent markers in a range of colors

 Craft knife

 Black acrylic paint and paintbrush

 Strong glue

 Masking tape

Step 1

Begin by drawing a circle on the bottom of the cup ¼in (6mm) in from the rim. Use a craft knife to cut this out.

Step 2

Paint the inside of the cup and cardboard tube black and leave to dry. You may need several coats to get an even coverage.

Step 3

On your sheet of acetate, draw around the end of the tube and cut out. Draw a little seascape image onto the acetate circle using permanent markers.

Step 4

Use strong glue to stick the seascape inside the bottom of the cup. Leave to dry.

Step 5

Use masking tape to attach the tube onto the bottom of the cup.

Step 6

Paint the outside of the telescope black and leave to dry.

Step 7

Cut three ½in (1cm) wide strips of gold card long enough to fit around the top, middle and bottom of the telescope (with a slight overlap). Glue in place on the telescope.

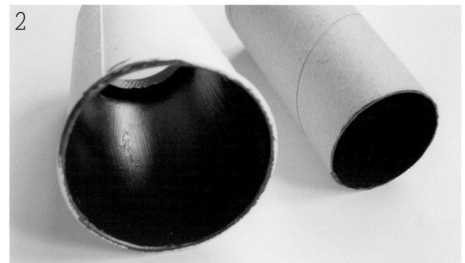

4

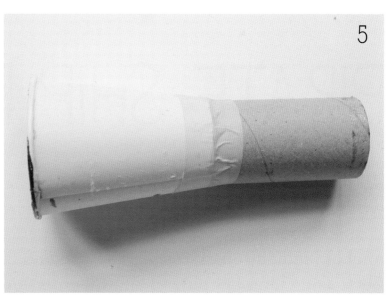

5

6

This telescope features a picture of a handsome ship, but you could draw a desert island, buried treasure, or even your own pirate crew.

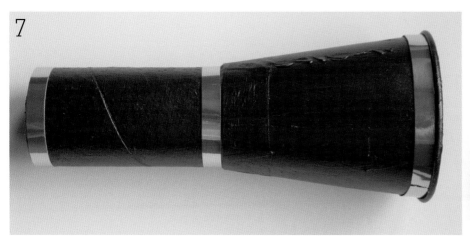

7

PIRATE SHIP PEN POT

All pirates like to keep a pen pot handy to help them draw their treasure maps, write in their captain's log, and pen letters home to their pirate parents. This one is made from plaster of Paris. It's extra special because it comes complete with an anchor (actually an eraser) and a skull and crossbones sail (which is a notepad). Set it aside for a few days to allow the plaster to dry out fully before decorating.

You will need

 2 x sheets of acetate, 12in (30cm) square

 1 x cardboard box, about 4 x 3 x 1½in (10 x 8 x 4cm); a small cereal box works well

 2 x cardboard tubes, about 5½in (14cm) long

 2¼lb (1kg) plaster of Paris

 About 2 cups of lentils (or similar, for weight)

 2 x lengths of dowel, about 10 x ¼in (25cm x 6mm)

 Scrap of corrugated card

 4 x cocktail sticks

 1 x plain pocket notepad, 3 x 4in (7 x 10cm)

 1 x sheet of black card, 8 x 12in (20 x 30cm)

 Scrap of white paper

 Scraps of black and white card

 Masking tape

 Scissors and craft knife

 Pliers

 Pencil

 Brown, black, gray, red, and green acrylic paints and paintbrushes

 Strong glue

 Coloring pens

 Plain white eraser measuring at least 2 x 1in (5 x 2.5cm)

 Black embroidery thread

Step 1

Use the template from page 63 to cut the mold from the acetate sheets; it will not fit on one sheet, so cut it in separate pieces and attach with masking tape. Fold up the sides where indicated to form a boat shape and tape together with masking tape. Make sure there are no gaps, or the plaster of Paris will leak out.

Step 2

Cut the top off the narrow end of the small box, then cover the remaining part of the box in masking tape. Repeat for the cardboard tubes, covering one end and both sides. Make sure there are no gaps.

Step 3

Mix up the plaster of Paris with water, following the manufacturer's instructions. Mix it up in small batches, using two cups of powder to one cup of water. Mix it well to remove lumps and tap the sides to release any air bubbles, then pour it into the boat mold. Repeat this until the mixture fills up two-thirds of the mold.

Step 4

Pour the lentils into the box and tubes, then insert them into the mixture, evenly spaced, with the box in the center. Tape them to the outside of the mold to keep them in place while the plaster sets.

Step 5

After 15 minutes, press the two pieces of dowel into the plaster, in between the tubes and the box. The dowels should stand up by themselves—just make sure they are straight! Leave to harden overnight.

Step 6

Remove the tape and peel off the acetate mold. Tip out the lentils and use pliers to twist out the cardboard tubes and boxes. Leave to dry out completely for two days.

Step 7

Paint the boat brown and leave to dry. Mark in pencil and paint any decorative finishes you want on the boat. This one has black portholes, a red and green border and a dark brown plank on the top.

Step 8

For the ship's wheel, draw a 1½in (4cm) circle onto corrugated card. Draw another circle, ½in (1cm) smaller, inside the first one, then cut out. Insert the cocktail sticks through the corrugations in the card to cross through one side of the circle to another, equally spaced apart. Paint this gray and glue inside the pot towards the front of the boat.

Step 9

For the sail, cover a notepad in black card on the front and back. Draw and color in your sail design onto white paper and cut out, then glue it onto the front of the notepad. Open the back cover and glue the notepad onto the front mast on the boat.

Step 10

Cut out the anchor template from page 63 and place it on top of the eraser. Draw around it, then use a craft knife to carefully cut out the shape; the eraser should be fairly soft. Use the tip of some sharp scissors to push out the hole. Thread black embroidery thread through the hole and glue the other end inside one of the pots on the boat.

Step 11

Finally, for the bunting, cut 10 to 12 1½in (4cm) diamond shapes from black and white scraps of card. Fold over and glue onto a 12in (30cm) piece of black embroidery thread.

Step 12

Glue one end of the bunting onto the sail, the other onto the back of the boat, and the middle onto the mast.

Keep children away from the plaster of Paris while it is being mixed and left to harden. The mixture will heat up a bit once it is hardening, so be careful when handling it.

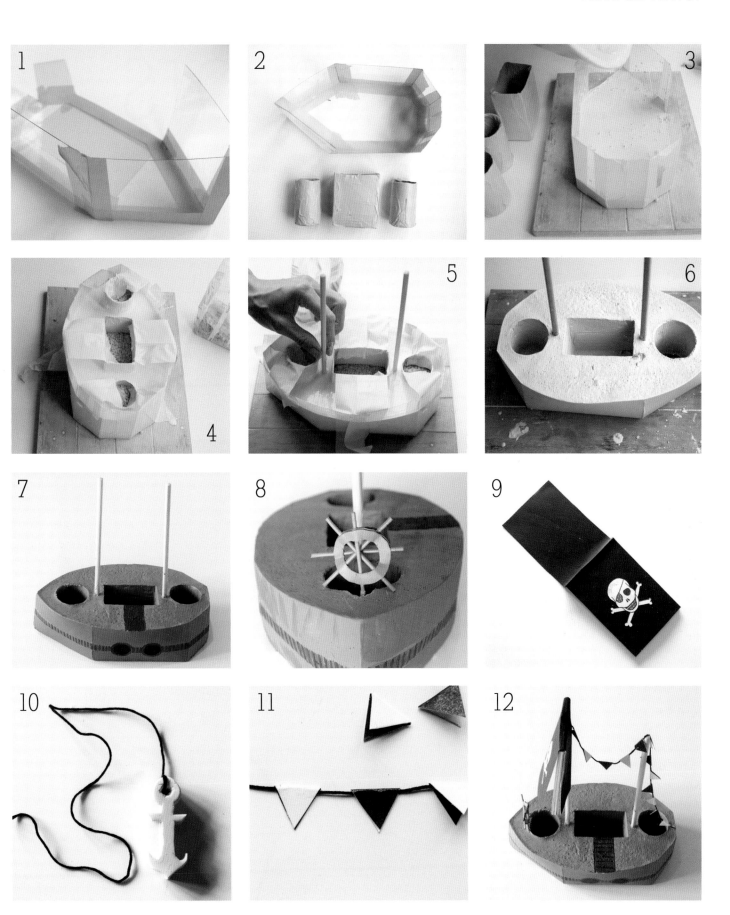

BUCCANEER BOOTS

These boots are an easy upcycling project using a pair of old wellies covered with black duct tape and a gold buckle. You could use black wellies if you have them without duct tape, but the embellishments are less likely to stick—and they will still tend to look like wellies at the end!

You will need

 Pair of wellington boots

 1 sheet of black craft foam 12 x 16in (30 x 40cm)

 47in (120cm) length of red ribbon, ¼in (6mm) thick

 Scraps of gold craft foam

 Roll of 2in (5cm) wide duct tape

 Scissors

 Pencil

 Single hole punch

 Double-sided tape

Step 1

Wrap a strip of duct tape over the toe end of the boots. Pinch the excess corners of tape together tightly and snip them off to create a neat edge.

Step 2

Continue to cover the boots with the tape—cut small slits around any curved parts if the duct tape doesn't sit flat.

Step 3

For the top of the boots, add a strip of tape around the top that sits halfway above the edge of the boot.

Step 4

Cut slits into the excess tape, fold it over and press inside the boot.

Step 5

Use the template on page 62 to cut out two black foam cuffs. Make two pencil marks on each end, ½in (1cm) from the edge and ½in (1cm) from both the top and bottom. Use a hole punch to make a hole through each mark.

Step 6

Use double-sided tape to attach the foam cuff to the top of the boots, with the top edges lined up. The ends should meet at the back.

Step 7

Cut the ribbon in half and thread it through the holes in the cuff like a shoelace. Tie in a bow to secure.

Step 8

For the straps, cut two strips of foam measuring 10 x 1½in (25 x 4cm). Trim one end on each piece to create a curved edge. Use the hole punch to make four holes, about ½in (1cm) from the edge and ½in (1cm) apart.

Step 9

Cut two buckle shapes from gold craft foam using the template on page 62. Slide them onto the strap about ¾in (2cm) from the end. Use double-sided tape to attach the straps around the top of the foot of the boot, with the buckles on the outside over the ankle.

CUTLASS AND BELT

This sturdy cardboard cutlass is great for fending off pesky rival pirates trying to steal treasure. It comes with a handy fabric belt to hold the cutlass.

You will need

 2 x pieces of corrugated card, about 18in (45cm) square

 15in (38cm) length of 1/16in (1.5mm) thick wire

 About 11ft (3.3m) of green string

 Scrap of fabric for belt (see Step 8 for measurements)

 1 x gold button, 3/4in (2cm) in diameter

 Marker pen

 Scissors

 Strong glue

 Silver duct tape

 Wire cutters

 Black duct tape

 Double-sided tape

 Sewing machine, matching thread and pins

 Iron and ironing board

 Sewing needle

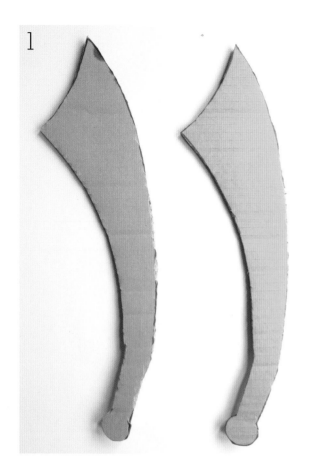

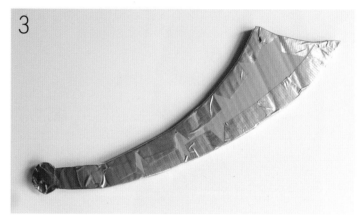

Step 1

Place the template from page 64 onto the corrugated card, draw around it and cut it out. Repeat to create two cutlass shapes.

Step 2

Spread glue onto one of the pieces of card and glue the other one on top. Leave to dry.

Step 3

Place a strip of silver duct tape along the long edge of the cutlass. Cut small tabs, 1in (2.5cm) apart, along the edge of the tape and fold over; the tabs will prevent the tape from puckering around the curved edge. Repeat for all the other edges.

Step 4

Attach strips of duct tape down the front and back of the cutlass and trim off any excess from the edges.

Step 5

Use wire cutters to wrap the end of the wire twice around the handle to secure it in place, 1in (2.5cm) from the end. Bend it over and wrap it around again, about 4in (10cm) from where you started. Snip off the excess wire, then cover with silver duct tape where it folds over the card to conceal any sharp edges.

Step 6

Wrap black duct tape all the way around the wire handle.

Step 7

Wrap double-sided tape around the cutlass in between the handle. Peel off the backing and wrap the green string over the tape, nice and tightly. Put a dab of strong glue onto both ends of the string to secure it in place.

Step 8

Measure your child's waist for the belt. The belt should hang loosely, so take this into account when taking the measurement. Add an additional 2in (5cm) to this measurement. Cut a 6in (15cm)-wide strip of fabric to this length.

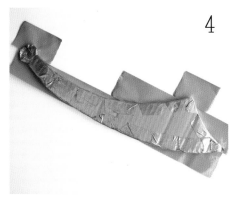

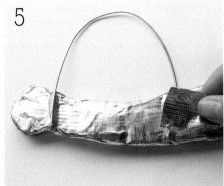

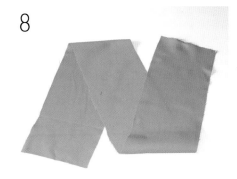

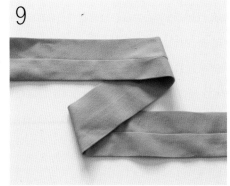

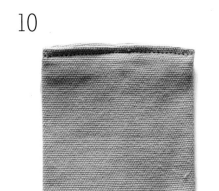

Step 9

Fold the fabric in half lengthways. Pin and sew along the edge with a ½in (1cm) seam allowance. Turn the fabric the right way out and press with the seam running down the center.

Step 10

Turn under each end by ½in (1cm). Pin and sew just inside the fold to hide the raw edges.

Step 11

Sew the button onto the belt, 1in (2.5cm) from one end. Then mark a buttonhole 1in (2.5cm) from the opposite end and cut a slit the same length as the button. Sew the buttonhole by machine or hand. To hand sew, carefully blanket stitch (see page 51) around the raw edges.

FISH FOR LOOT GAME

This game teaches children balance, dexterity, and numeracy skills by enabling them to hook pirate shapes out of the sea with a rod. Each shape has a score, so play with a few shipmates and see who can tot up the most points. All you need to do is throw your shapes overboard (or off the edge of a sofa...) and prepare to fish for treasure.

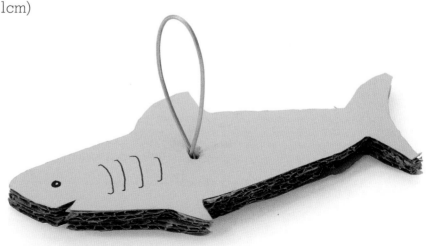

You will need

- 1 x piece of corrugated cardboard, about 24 x 24in (60 x 60cm)

- 2 x sheets of silver card, 8 x 12in (20 x 30cm)

- 1 x sheet each of gold, gray, green, and white card, 8 x 12in (20 x 30cm)

- Reel of ¹⁄₁₆in (1.5mm) thick wire

- 1 x length of dowel, 24 x ½in (60 x 1cm)

- Black marker pen

- Scissors

- Glue stick

- Wire cutters

- Masking tape

- Gold and black duct tape

Step 1

Use the templates on page 63 to draw and cut out the shapes from corrugated card. Cut 10 coins and 4 skulls, sharks, and bottles. Then use the templates to cut the following from the colored card:
• 4 x green bottles
• 4 x white skulls
• 4 x gray sharks
• 6 x silver coins
• 4 x gold coins.

Step 2

For each item you will need two pieces of corrugated card and two pieces of colored card. Carefully line up and glue the corrugated pieces together in pairs. Then glue one of the corresponding colored card pieces on top.

Step 3

Draw detail onto the shapes in black pen—you can use the templates for guidance.

Step 4

Add different numbers to each of the coins.

Step 5

Use a pair of scissors to push a hole through the shape, from the colored card side. Using wire cutters, cut 10 lengths of wire, each measuring 8in (20cm). Bend the wire in half and twist the ends together. Fold in the center to create a right angle and insert the ends into the hole in the shape.

Step 6

Tape the ends of the wire down using masking tape.

Step 7

Glue the other piece of colored card over the top of the wire to seal it in.

Step 8

On the bases of the shapes (apart from the coins), draw numbers ranging from 1 to 10 in black pen to create scores.

Step 9

To make the hook, cut 10in (25cm) of wire using wire cutters and fold it in half, pressing closed with the blunt edge of the wire cutters. Use the cutters to bend the end into a hook shape.

Step 10

Attach the hook onto the end of the dowel using gold duct tape. Wrap black duct tape around the rest of the dowel.

To play, simply take it in turns to hook the shapes out of the water. Keep hold of your loot and tally up the totals at the end. The winner is the player with the most points. To make it a real challenge, you could wear an eye patch or a blindfold and then try to hook the shapes.

You don't just have to stick to the templates in this book—try creating your own pirate shapes to fish for. An old pair of boots, a parrot, a telescope, or a pirate hat would work well.

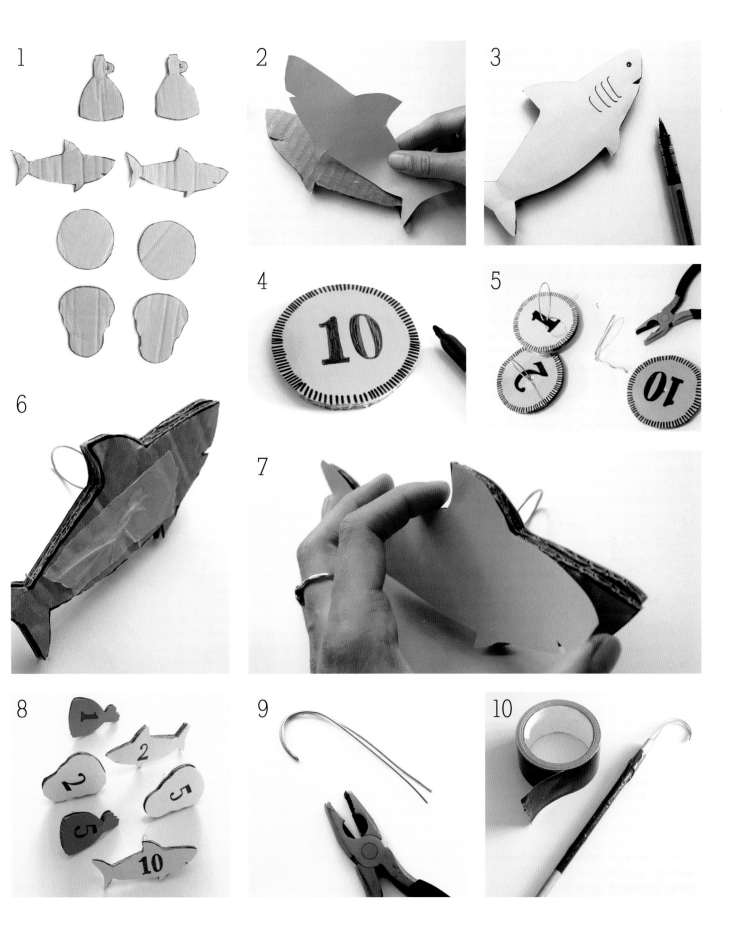

EASY-SEW WAISTCOAT

This little waistcoat is a one-size-fits-all (all kids, that is!) super-easy sewing project. Bias binding is added to finish the edges. Adding binding to the tuck on the back can be a little fiddly, so if you are a novice sewer follow the dotted line on the template to avoid the tuck. Pair with a stripy T-shirt for the best pirate effect.

You will need

 20in (50cm) square of black cotton fabric

 13ft (4m) of red bias binding tape

 About 12in (30cm) square of fusible webbing

 About 12in (30cm) square of white cotton

 6 x gold buttons, ¾in (2cm) in diameter

 Scissors

 Sewing machine, matching thread and pins

 Iron and ironing board

 Pencil

 Tape measure

 Optional: 1½in (4cm) piece of black Velcro/ hook-and-loop tape (hook side)

Step 1

Cut out the pattern pieces from page 64. Fold the fabric and use the pattern to cut two front pieces and one back piece from the black fabric. Place the back piece along the fold of the fabric where indicated.

Step 2

Pin the front and back pieces together at the shoulders and side seams and sew with a ½in (1cm) seam allowance.

Step 3

Open up the bias binding and line up the edge with the bottom of the waistcoat, on the wrong side of the fabric.

Step 4

Pin all the way along, going round the tuck in the center if you have opted to sew it (this is a little fiddly) to the end. Sew along the fold in the binding.

Step 5

Fold the binding over the fabric, then pin and sew in place on the right side of the waistcoat along the center of the binding. The binding should enclose the raw edges of the fabric.

Step 6

Repeat for the side panels—start from one bottom corner of the waistcoat and sew all the way around the neckline to the other corner.

Step 7

Trim the edges of the binding when you reach the other side so that it is neat against the bottom.

Step 8

Repeat for the armholes, leaving ½in (1cm) excess at the end of the binding to overlap a little.

Step 9

Iron the fusible webbing onto the white fabric to glue them together. Use the template on page 64 to cut two bones from the fabric. Remove the backing from the webbing and line up to form a cross on the back of the waistcoat. Iron this in place.

Step 10

Measure and mark in pencil three evenly spaced points along both sides of the waistcoat, ¾in (2cm) from the edge. Sew the gold buttons in place.

OPTIONAL: If you want to create a little perch for Polly Parrot (page 4) on the waistcoat, sew a square of Velcro onto the shoulder.

JOLLY ROGER FLAG

A flag is essential for claiming treasure and displaying in your boat to make sure no one dares come near your beautiful vessel. This one is a rather friendly Roger, and he's easy to stitch with a little embroidery thread decoration. The edges of the flag have been left unsewn for a raggedy look; if you want to be a neater pirate, you could fold these over and sew before making the channel for the pole.

You will need

 12 x 15in (30 x 38cm) black cotton fabric

 8 x 6in (20 x 15cm) white cotton fabric

 9 x 5in (23 x 13cm) red and white spotted cotton fabric

 1 x piece of fusible webbing, about 10in (25cm) square

 1 x length of dowel, 30 x ½in (75 x 1cm)

 Sewing machine, black sewing thread, and pins

 Iron and ironing board

 Pencil

 Black, white, and red embroidery thread and needle

 Red acrylic paint and paintbrush

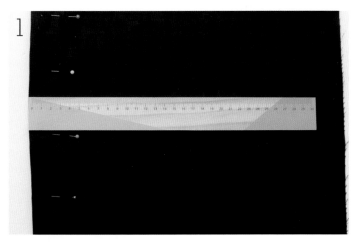

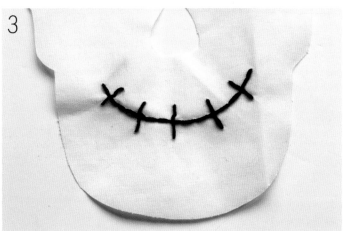

Step 1

To create the channel for the flagpole, fold over one of the short sides of the black fabric by 1⅜in (3.5cm), pin to secure and sew down the edge. Also sew along the top of the channel along the edge to seal one end.

Step 2

Use the templates on page 64 to cut out a skull from white fabric and fusible webbing, and a hat from red and white spotted fabric and webbing. Iron the webbing onto the back of the skull and hat.

Step 3

Use a pencil to lightly draw a mouth shape onto the skull, as shown on the template. Knot a length of black embroidery thread and hand sew on the mouth, using backstitch (see box on opposite page).

Step 4

Place the skull in the center of the flag and iron in place as per the manufacturer's instructions. Line up the hat and press that on too.

Step 5

Use white embroidery thread to blanket stitch (see box on opposite page) around the edges of the skull and inside the eye socket and nose. Use red thread to blanket stitch around the hat.

Step 6

Paint the piece of dowel red and leave to dry. Slide the flag onto the pole and get ready to set sail!

5

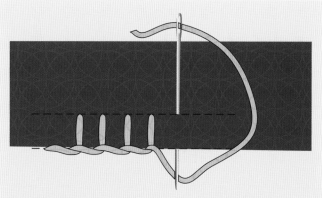

Blanket stitch

Bring your needle out through the very edge of
the fabric. Insert your needle back into the fabric a
little way to the right and the same distance in from
the edge. Make sure the thread is under the needle
tip before pulling it through.

Make the next stitch in the same way to the right
of the first and continue, making sure the vertical
stitches are all the same length and the same
distance apart.

6

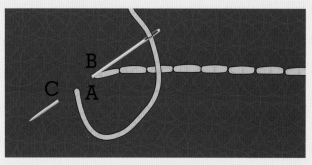

Backstitch

Backstitch is excellent for creating a straight line.
Using the illustration as a guide, bring your needle
up through the fabric at A and then push the needle
back down at B. Bring the needle up again at C, and
then down again at A. Work along like this to create
a neat continuous line.

PIRATE SHIP

There are many ways to build a boat, and you can adapt yours to suit the materials you have available. The more boxes you can find, the bigger your boat can be, and the more shipmates you can fit on deck. Bear in mind, though, that the boat will decrease in sturdiness the bigger it gets! Outlined below are some top tips for how to create the best pirate ship.

Useful materials

 3–4 large cardboard boxes and scraps of corrugated card

 Yoghurt pot or large plastic lid

 Paper plates

 Sheets of acetate

 Selection of bottle tops for buttons

 Broom handle or long length of dowel

 Terracotta plant pot with a hole in the base for the broom handle or piece of dowel

 Bunting and old sheets for sail and sea

 Felt

 Colorful duct tape

 Scissors and craft knife

 Glue

 Felt-tip pens

 Gold and silver acrylic paints and paintbrushes

 Washing detergent bottle lid

 Large dinner plate

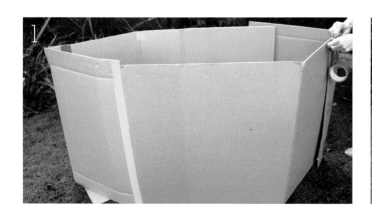

Step 1

Cut open two or three large cardboard boxes, then reassemble them to form a ship shape with narrower pointed ends. Tape in place with plenty of duct tape.

Step 2

Cut a door into one side of the boat. Add a handle by sticking on a yoghurt pot or large lid (laundry detergent lids work well).

Step 3

To be able to fold the boat away for storage, make the base as a separate section that can be pulled out when playtime is over. You can draw around the boat onto a large sheet of card (or several smaller ones taped together) and cut this out.

Step 4

Portholes can be made by cutting holes in the side of the box, just smaller than a paper plate. For each porthole, cut away the center of a paper plate and replace with a piece of acetate to look like glass. Glue this onto the holes and decorate with bolts using felt-tip pens.

Step 5

Bottle tops of all shapes and sizes make great buttons for a control panel. Ones with flip-up caps or twisting nozzles work best for playing with. Stick them onto a small piece of cardboard and attach inside the boat.

Step 6

To create a plank, cut a long strip of cardboard and tape it inside the boat, coming out through the door. It can then be folded up inside the boat when not in use.

Step 7

A broom handle or long piece of dowel sitting inside an upturned terracotta plant pot makes an excellent mast. It can be adorned with bunting or an old sheet for a sail.

Step 8

Surround the boat with an old blue bedsheet to create the sea. Cut shark fins or crocodiles from cardboard and throw them into the sea to create infested waters.

Step 9

To make an anchor, cut out two anchor shapes from corrugated card and glue them together. Glue on bottle tops, painted gold or copper as decoration. Make a chain by gluing or sewing strips of felt into loops in a chain, then glue the chain onto the boat.

Step 10

Make a helm for your ship by drawing around a large dinner plate onto a piece of corrugated card. Draw another circle, 1½in (4cm) smaller, inside. Add 1½in (4cm) wide strips of card across the circles to create handles—they should come about 4in (10cm) out from the edge of the circle. Cut out and paint silver. Draw around a large washing detergent bottle lid (one with an inner and outer rim) in the center and cut out, then insert the lid through the middle of the wheel and glue onto the boat. The wheel should spin freely around the lid.

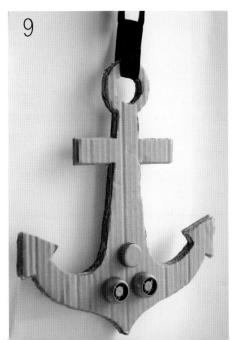

PIRATE PARTY

Now that you've decked out your little pirate from head to toe, it's time to create the ultimate jamboree. This section will provide you with loads of great ideas for pirate-themed food, décor, games and activities.

Treasure Map Invites

Cut jagged edges into a piece of paper, then draw on a map of your house, complete with treasure, crocodiles, or sharks. Add party details in the form of a key in one corner. Roll it up into a scroll and tie it with ribbon.

Décor

TABLE DECORATIONS

Lay out a blue tablecloth and decorate with napkins folded into little boat shapes, little cardboard islands, crocodiles, and treasure chests—small boxes filled with little sweets or biscuits.

BOAT SHOWSTOPPER

Make a boat from a couple of large cardboard boxes (see page 52).

SANDPIT TREASURE ISLAND

If you have a sandpit, you can set it up as a desert island. Bury gold coins, cheap jewelry, and plastic creepy crawlies for little pirates to hunt for. You can even spray some pebbles with gold paint and dot them around to make gold nuggets.

Party Nibbles

JELLY OCEAN

Make pirate ships by cutting oranges into segments and inserting cocktail sticks with pirate flags into them. Mix up some blue jelly and pour into a glass bowl, then add sweetie fishes and put the pirate ships on top.

SKULL AND CROSSBONES COOKIES

Make a batch of cookies cut out with a skull cookie cutter (available online or in cake shops). Cover in white ready-to-roll icing (using the cutter), and draw a face in edible writing pens.

TREASURE MAP PIZZAS

Cut pizza dough into rectangles, add a tomato base and cheese, then use vegetables to mark out a treasure map. Mark out a route using cut-up black olives and green pepper palm trees.

BAGUETTE BOATS

Cut small baguettes in half lengthways and add toppings. Pop a cocktail stick in the middle with a sail.

HIDDEN TREASURE CUPCAKES

Make cupcakes and cut the tops off. Scoop out a little of the sponge in the middle and fill with edible treats. Then pop the top back on and add icing and decorations on top.

Pirate Games

PIN THE POLLY ON THE PIRATE

Draw a handsome pirate onto cardboard and make a separate Pretty Polly. Then blindfold pirates in turn and see who can pin the Polly nearest to the shoulder of the captain, using adhesive putty.

PIRATE ASSAULT COURSE

Turn your garden or house into a pirate training camp. Put the children into teams and set them challenges such as walking the plank, jumping over sharks, or firing beanbag cannonballs at cardboard crocodiles.

TREASURE HUNT

Bury a small shoebox decorated to look like a chest (see page 12) and fill it with goodies such as chocolate coins. Draw a treasure map and mark on an X. Older children can be given clues.

Pirate Activities

PIRATE PHOTO BOOTH

Fill a box with pirate clothes and accessories for pirates to have their photos taken in. Cut cardboard beards, hats, and parrots from cardboard and stick onto pieces of dowel for pirates to pose with.

TREASURE CHEST CAKE

This treasure chest cake is the gold at the end of a pirate party. It's surprisingly simple to make from chocolate sponge, a little buttercream, and some edible treasure! Your hungry little pirates will do a merry jig when they see it.

You will need

For the sponge:

- 2 deep rectangular cake tins, about 10 x 7in (25 x 18cm)
- 1lb 9oz (700g) butter, at room temperature
- 1lb 9oz (700g) golden caster sugar
- 14 eggs
- 23oz (650g) self-raising flour (sifted)
- 2 tsp baking powder
- 2½oz (70g) cocoa powder
- 7fl oz (200ml) milk
- 2 tsp vanilla essence

To decorate:

- 1lb 12oz (800g) chocolate buttercream
- About 7oz (200g) plain buttercream
- About 3½oz (100g) each of black and yellow fondant icing
- 1 packet round sandwich cookies
- Edible gold paint and paintbrush
- Rice paper
- Edible ink pens
- Edible jewels, necklaces, shoelaces, etc
- About 14oz (400g) golden caster sugar

Supplies:

- 3 or 4 cake dowels
- Matches
- Cling film
- Large cake board

Step 1

Preheat the oven to 325°F (170°C).
Cream the butter and sugar together.
Gradually beat in the eggs, then
fold in the flour, cocoa, and baking
powder. Mix in the milk and the
vanilla essence.

Step 2

Grease and line the tins and divide
the batter between the two. Bake
for 40–50 minutes or until a skewer
inserted into the center comes out
clean. Remove from the oven and
let the cakes cool completely. You
can wrap them in cling film and pop
them in the freezer if you want to
make the sponge in advance.

Step 3

Use a bread knife to slice off the very
top from one of the cakes so that it is
flat. Round off both the long sides to
create curved edges and set aside—
this will become the lid of your cake.
For the base, mark 1in (2.5cm) from
the edge on the top of the cake, all
the way around. Cut along this line,
going about halfway to the bottom of
the cake. Scoop out the middle (you
don't need to be too neat as this will
be covered with treasure!).

Step 4

Cover the two cakes with a thin layer
of chocolate buttercream. Cut two
lengths of dowel to measure 3.5in
(9cm) and another two to measure
5in (12.5cm). Place the base cake
on the board and push the shorter
dowels into the corners at the back
of the cake, and the longer pieces a
couple of inches down on the sides.

Step 5

Take the other cake and place it
on top, pushing it partly into the
dowels to hold it in place. It should
look like the lid of the box is open.
If your cake needs it, you could add
another dowel in the middle of the
chest for extra strength. Add more
buttercream to the cake, smoothing
over with a palette knife.

Step 6

To make the straps, roll the black
fondant out between two sheets of
cling film. Cut the fondant into two
1in (2.5cm) wide strips and round
one end of both. Place on the lid of
the cake with the rounded ends just
hanging over the edge.

Step 7

To make the buckles, roll out the yellow
fondant between two sheets of cling
film. Cut a 1in (2.5cm) square out and
another square about ½ inch (1cm)
bigger around it. Add a small rectangle
of fondant to the center to make the
middle of the buckle. Press the buckles
in place on the straps. Cut small triangle
out of the remaining yellow fondant to
put on the corners of the chest.

Step 8

Paint the cookies with the edible gold
paint to look like coins. Fill the cake
with the coins, jewels, and gems. The
cake should be pretty full to help
hold the lid up. Try to hide the dowels
with the treasure if you can.

Step 9

To make the 'sand', spread plain
buttercream roughly onto the board
around the cake and sprinkle golden
caster sugar liberally over the top.

Step 10

Finally, for the treasure map, cut a
7in (18cm) square of rice paper. Use
edible ink to draw on a map, then
burn the edges with a match for an
authentic look.

TEMPLATES

Templates that are shown at actual size can be traced and cut out, or photocopied. For templates that have been reduced in size, enlarge them on a photocopier to the percentage stated. Align each template as near to the top left-hand corner of the photocopier glass as possible. You may need to repeat this a few times to find the best position.

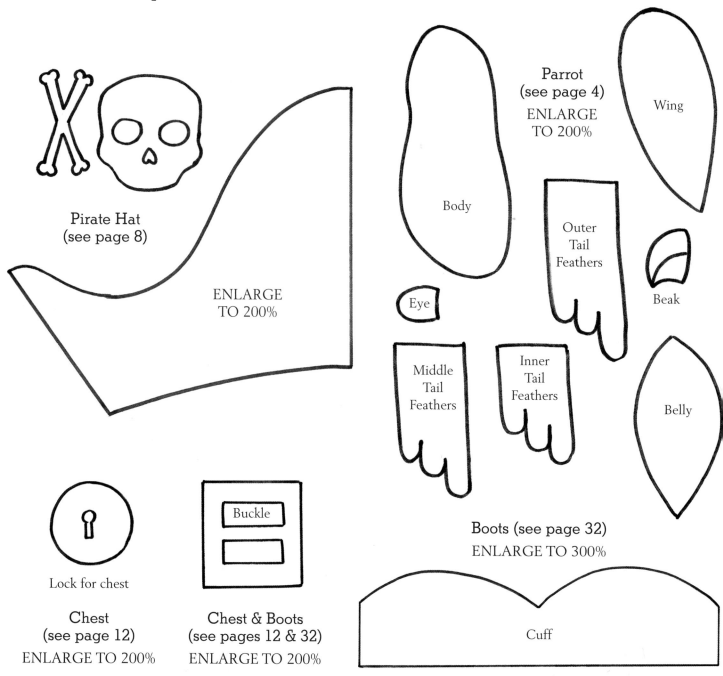

Pirate Hat
(see page 8)

ENLARGE
TO 200%

Parrot
(see page 4)
ENLARGE
TO 200%

Wing

Body

Outer
Tail
Feathers

Beak

Eye

Middle
Tail
Feathers

Inner
Tail
Feathers

Belly

Buckle

Lock for chest

Chest
(see page 12)
ENLARGE TO 200%

Chest & Boots
(see pages 12 & 32)
ENLARGE TO 200%

Boots (see page 32)
ENLARGE TO 300%

Cuff

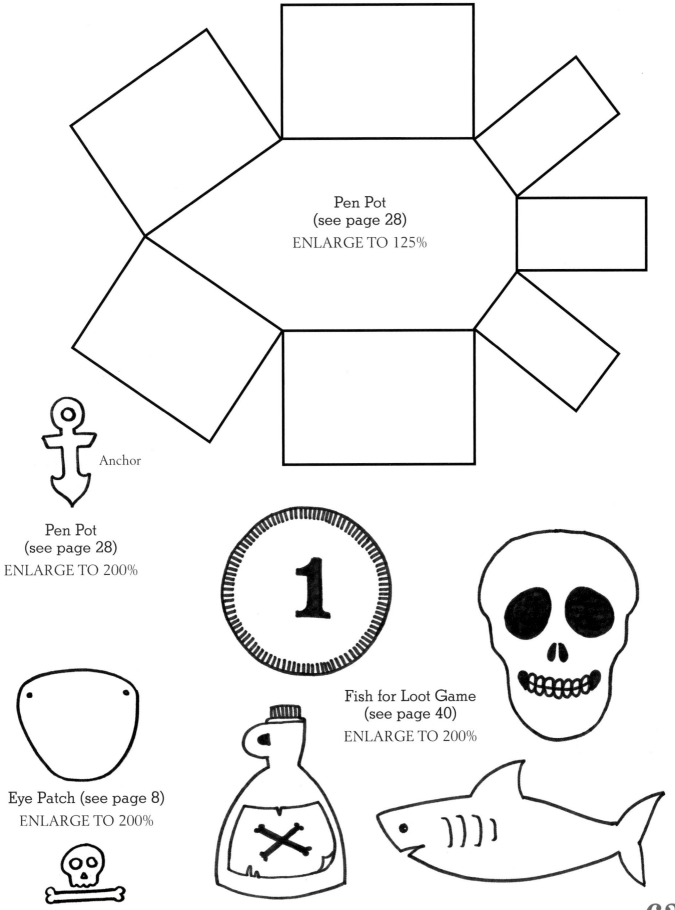

Pen Pot
(see page 28)
ENLARGE TO 125%

Anchor

Pen Pot
(see page 28)
ENLARGE TO 200%

1

Fish for Loot Game
(see page 40)
ENLARGE TO 200%

Eye Patch (see page 8)
ENLARGE TO 200%

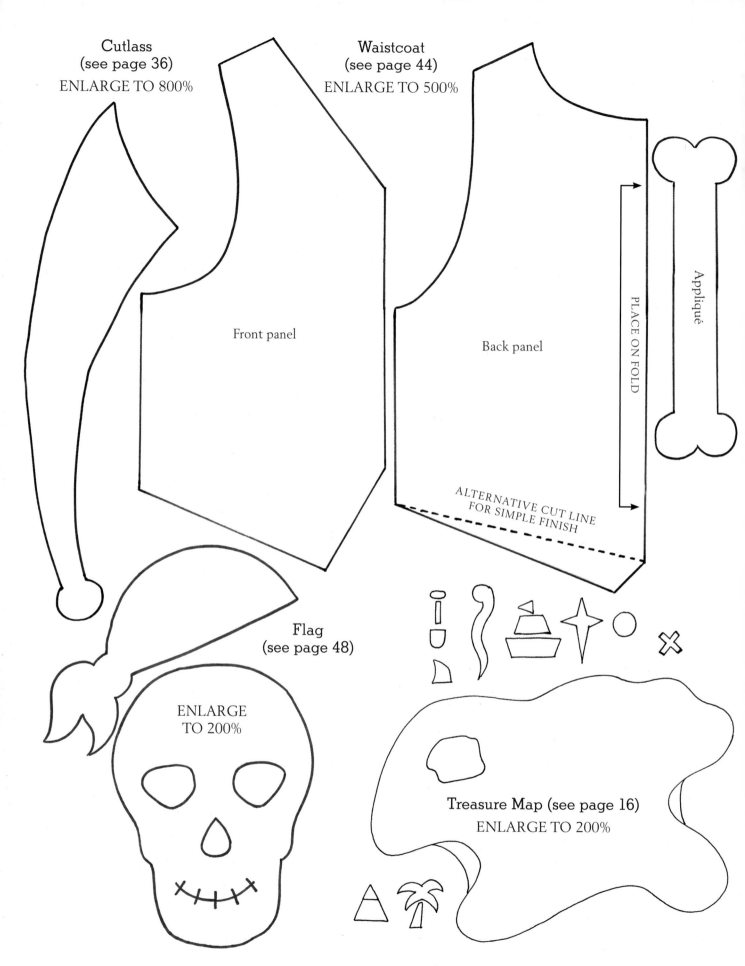

Cutlass
(see page 36)
ENLARGE TO 800%

Waistcoat
(see page 44)
ENLARGE TO 500%

Front panel

Back panel

Appliqué

PLACE ON FOLD

ALTERNATIVE CUT LINE
FOR SIMPLE FINISH

Flag
(see page 48)

ENLARGE
TO 200%

Treasure Map (see page 16)
ENLARGE TO 200%

To place an Order, or to request a catalog, contact: GMC Publications Ltd, Castle Place, 166 High Street, Lewes, East Sussex, BN7 1XU, United Kingdom

Tel: +44 (0)1273 488005   www.gmcbooks.com